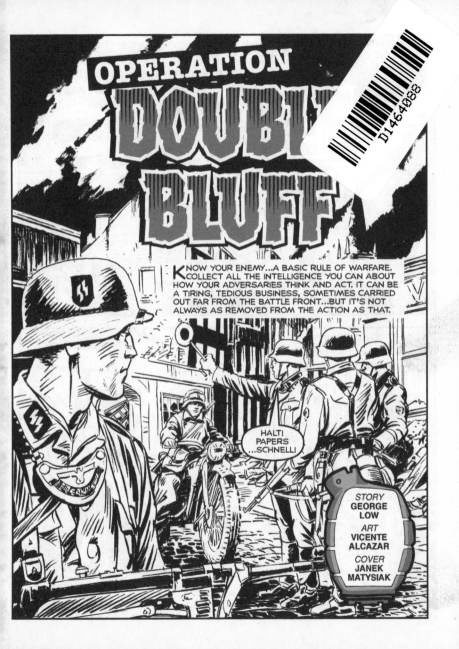

1944. THE INVADING ALLIES WERE PUNCHING THEIR WAY OUT OF FRANCE TO SPREAD INTO NEIGHBOURING COUNTRIES. THINGS WERE TENSE IN THIS GERMAN-CONTROLLED AREA OF THE NETHERLANDS WHICH HAD ALREADY BEEN BOMBED AND SHELLED.

SO YOUR UNIT HAS BEEN HIT HARD? NOT THINKING OF SLIPPING AWAY HOME, ARE YOU?

IF ONLY I COULD, BUT MUNICH IS TOO FAR, FELDWEBEL. I BET YOU WERE WISHING YOU WERE THERE TOO IF I'VE PLACED YOUR ACCENT RIGHT.

AS HE FOUND ALL TO BE IN ORDER WITH THE SOLDIER'S PAPERS, THE FLINT-FACED FIELD POLICE SERGEANT ALLOWED A GRIMACE WHICH PASSED AS A SMILE TO CREASE HIS FACE.

JA, IT WOULD BE GOOD TO FISH IN THE ISAR AGAIN, BUT GET MOVING NOW...AND DON'T ACT SO SMART IN FUTURE.

ON MY WAY, FELDWEBEL. MAYBE WE'LL MEET IN THE MARIENPLATZ SOME DAY.

THE MOTORCYCLIST EASED ON HIS WAY BUT STOPPED AROUND THE NEXT CORNER WHERE ANOTHER MAN IN FIELD GREY STEPPED FROM THE SHADOWS.

YOU HAD ME WORRIED FOR A SECOND THERE WITH THAT CHIT-CHAT, KAMERAD.

RELAX, IT WAS ALL IN HAND, BUT I DON'T WANT TO HANG ABOUT ANY LONGER EITHER.

BY DAWN THE BIKE-BORNE PAIR HAD REACHED THEIR RENDEZVOUS WHERE A BRITISH ARMY OFFICER CALMLY AWAITED THEM.

GLAD YOU'RE BACK IN ONE PIECE.

NOT AS MUCH AS WE ARE, SIR.

THEY WERE SPEAKING ENGLISH NOW BECAUSE THE TWO "GERMANS" WERE IN FACT MEMBERS OF THE BRITISH INTELLIGENCE CORPS WHO HAD BEEN SENT BEHIND ENEMY LINES IN DISGUISE TO LEARN WHAT THEY COULD.

FIRST IMPRESSIONS THEN?

JERRY IS STILL FULL OF FIGHT ON THE WHOLE, BUT CRACKS ARE BEGINNING TO APPEAR.

AMMO AND FOOD ISN'T GETTING FORWARD AS QUICK AS THEY WOULD LIKE, SIR.

LIEUTENANT ALFRED TAIT WAS WELL PLEASED WITH THE WORK OF SERGEANT COLIN BRADY AND CORPORAL MIKE MEACH. ALL THREE WERE FLUENT GERMAN SPEAKERS AND MIKE HAD THE ADVANTAGE OF A GERMAN MOTHER WHO HAILED FROM MUNICH.

PIECE OF LUCK THAT THE FIELD POLICE N.C.O. CAME FROM THAT NECK OF THE WOODS TOO.

THEY SAY YOU MAKE YOUR OWN LUCK, JUST LIKE WE COBBLE TOGETHER GOOD INTELLIGENCE.

A USEFUL COLLECTION OF NOTES ON TROOP MOVEMENTS, ANTI-AIRCRAFT GUN SITES AND GENERAL BACKGROUND GEN HAD BEEN AMASSED. NOW IT WAS TIME TO HEAD BACK AND ANALYSE IT ALL.

THE THREE INTELLIGENCE GATHERERS REACHED THEIR TEMPORARY, BOMB-BLASTED BASE TO CONDENSE THEIR GLUT OF GEN INTO A LOGICAL SUMMING UP.

WHAT WASN'T SO EASY TO ENVISAGE, HOWEVER, WAS THE AUDACIOUS ALLIED PLAN TO LAND PARATROOPERS AT ARNHEM IN ENEMY-OCCUPIED HOLLAND AND SEIZE VITAL BRIDGES OVER THE RIVER RHINE.

THE SKY IS JUST FULL OF PLANES, SIR.

JUST KEEP YOUR EYES ON YOUR CHART, NAVIGATOR. THIS IS NO TIME TO MESS UP.

PARATROOP REGIMENT LIEUTENANT RALPH LOACH DIDN'T INTEND TO SEE HIS SQUAD'S ROLE IN OPERATION "MARKET GARDEN" GO WRONG EITHER. HE HADN'T TASTED ACTION BEFORE AND WAS TRYING TO HIDE HIS FEAR OF WHAT LAY AHEAD.

NOT LONG TO GO NOW. YOU ALL KNOW WHAT NEEDS DONE AND WE DON'T WANT TO COME UP SHORT ON ANY OF IT.

LIKES THE SOUND OF HIS OWN VOICE DOES THE LIEUTENANT.

RALPH MEANT WELL, BUT EVEN THE NERVES HE HAD SUFFERED BEFORE HIS FIRST TRAINING JUMP HADN'T PREPARED HIM FOR FLYING INTO BATTLE...AND INTO ENEMY FIRE.

AAGH!

CURSE THE JERRIES!

REALISING A DAKOTA HAD BEEN HIT CLOSE BY, RALPH STRUGGLED TO CONTROL HIS RISING PANIC.

STICK TO ORDERS AND IT WILL WORK OUT FINE...

GERMAN GUNNERS, FULLY AWARE OF THE AIRBORNE ARMADA BY NOW, WERE ZEROING IN ON IT.

NO SHORTAGE OF TARGETS UP THERE TODAY!

DEADLY 88MM SHELLS ROSE FROM FAR BELOW. ONE CLIPPED THE WING TIP OF THE DOUGLAS DAKOTA IN WHICH RALPH AND HIS MEN SAT HUNCHED.

THE CONTROLS AREN'T RESPONDING! GET THOSE PARAS OUT OF THIS KITE ...FAST!

INSIDE THE DC3, DISCIPLINE HELD. WHAT MIGHT HAVE BEEN CHAOS WAS CONTROLLED BY THE ROYAL AIR FORCE DESPATCHER WHO URGED THE PARAS INTO THE VOID.

GREEN LIGHT...GO!

I DON'T THINK WE'RE ANYWHERE NEAR OUR DROPPING ZONE!

REGARDLESS OF WHAT LAY BELOW, SURVIVAL, RATHER THAN
REACHING THEIR DESIGNATED TARGETS, TOOK PRIORITY NOW.

MY FIRST OP
AND IT'S GOING
ALL WRONG!

THE OPERATION GOT A LOT WORSE WHEN THE DAMAGED TRANSPORT'S WING FRAME
BUCKLED THEN COLLAPSED UNDER THE STRAIN. THE PLANE TWISTED DOWNWARDS
WITH THE R.A.F. CREW AND SOME OF RALPH'S PARAS TRAPPED ON BOARD.

AAGH!

YE
GODS!

REELING IN SHOCK AT WHAT HE HAD SEEN, RALPH HAD TO CONCENTRATE ON LANDING BUT HIS 'CHUTE SNAGGED IN A TALL TREE AND HE WAS SLAMMED — HARD — INTO THE UNFORGIVING TRUNK.

BLAST IT! URRGH!

SOME OF THE FEW SURVIVORS WERE LUCKIER AND TOUCHED DOWN SAFELY. THE PRIORITY WAS TO SHRUG OFF THEIR 'CHUTES AND TAKE STOCK OF THEIR SITUATION.

FORM UP ON ME AS FAST AS YOU CAN!

ON MY WAY, CORP.

THE STRANDED MEN HAD BEEN DEALT A BAD HAND THAT DAY — A HAIL OF 7.92MM BULLETS PROVED TO BE A HARSH WELCOME TO ENEMY-HELD EUROPE.

A UNIT OF S.S. SOLDIERS, HEADING TOWARDS THE MAIN LANDING SITE, HAD CHANCED UPON THE PARA SQUAD AND EFFICIENTLY SURROUNDED THEM.

14

THE BRITISH TROOPS HAD LITTLE CHANCE OF ESCAPE, NEVER MIND VICTORY, YET THEY FOUGHT FIERCELY.

KEEP GOING!

AAGH!

THE LAST MAN STANDING FINALLY FELL.

AAGH!

THE FIRING HALTED. THE SILENCE THAT FELL WAS CUT BY THE VOICE OF THE S.S. MAJOR IN CHARGE OF THE SQUAD.

CHECK THE SCHWEIN FOR ANY SIGN OF LIFE.

THE SOUND OF THE SKIRMISH HAD FILTERED THROUGH TO RALPH AS HE WOOZILY RETURNED TO CONSCIOUSNESS.

GUNSHOTS... YELLING...THE LADS MUST HAVE RUN INTO JERRIES...

OF THE SQUAD WHICH HAD LEAPT CLEAR OF THE DOOMED DAKOTA WITH THE LIEUTENANT, ONLY A FEW STILL BREATHED. THEY WERE NOW BEING FINISHED OFF IN COLD BLOOD ON THE ORDER OF THE S.S. OFFICER

WIPE THEM OUT. LEAVE NONE OF THEM ALIVE!

16

THE MP40 IN THE FANATIC'S HANDS HAMMERED HOME A BURST OF BULLETS. RALPH CONVULSED AND WAS THROWN ABOUT LIKE A PUPPET ON A STRING.

WITHOUT A SECOND GLANCE AT ANY OF THE VICTIMS, THE RUTHLESS KILLERS MOVED ON TO CARRY OUT WHATEVER WAS REQUIRED TO DEFEND THEIR REICH.

URGH!

AUF WIEDERSEHEN, ENGLANDER!

LET THEM COME, AMERICANS, BRITISH, CANADIANS ...THEY'LL REGRET IT!

THE SKIRMISH HAD ATTRACTED THE ATTENTION OF TWO LOCAL DUTCHMEN. THOUGH THEY FEARED ENEMY REPRISALS, THAT DID NOT STOP THEM BRAVELY CUTTING RALPH FREE AND LUGGING HIM AWAY.

HE'S BREATHING ...JUST. MOST OF THE BULLETS SEEM TO HAVE HIT HIS HARNESS BUCKLE.

THAT WAS LUCKY, BUT WE'D BETTER GET HIM TO DOCTOR VAN RIJN FAST.

GUNSHOT WOUNDS HAD PLAYED LITTLE PART IN THE LOCAL DOCTOR'S ROUTINE BEFORE THE WAR, BUT HE TOOK ON THE CHALLENGE AND SOMEHOW KEPT HIS PATIENT ALIVE.

HIS FEVER HAS BROKEN, BUT HE NEEDS BETTER CARE THAN I CAN GIVE HIM. THE SOONER THE NAZIS RETREAT THE BETTER FOR ALL OF US.

RALPH RAGED AT REGULATIONS, BUT HE ALSO FELT SICK TO THE STOMACH FOR WHAT HAD HAPPENED TO HIS MEN AT THE HANDS OF THE SADISTIC S.S. OFFICER.

EVEN IF I NEVER DO ANYTHING ELSE, I WANT TO SETTLE THE SCORE WITH THAT NAZI. HIS FACE HAUNTS MY DREAMS, I'LL NEVER FORGET IT.

THAT THE ARNHEM OPERATION HAD NOT BEEN A GREAT SUCCESS PREYED ON HIS MIND TOO. IT HAD BEEN LAUNCHED WITH GREAT HOPE AND CONFIDENCE, BUT FULL DETAILS OF THE ENEMY STRENGTH...

...HAD APPARENTLY NOT REACHED THOSE WHO WERE TO DROP IN TO CARRY OUT THE MISSION.

OUR INTELLIGENCE BODS GOT IT WRONG. JERRY HAD HALF AN ARMY THERE.

BEHIND IT ALL, THOUGH, HE WAS NOT SURE HOW HE MIGHT HAVE MEASURED UP IN ACTION.

HMM. SHOT WITHOUT ONCE FIRING BACK! HOW PATHETIC IS THAT?

HIS FEAR THAT HE MIGHT NOT HAVE MADE THE GRADE, THEN SITTING AROUND WAITING AND WONDERING, GNAWED AT HIM. FINALLY AN OFFICIAL LETTER ARRIVED.

THIS COULD BE MY NEW ORDERS...AT LAST!

THE LETTER WAS INDEED HIS NEW ORDERS, BUT A POSTING TO AN INTELLIGENCE CORPS UNIT TO STUDY THEIR METHODS AND BROADEN HIS EXPERIENCE WAS NOT WELCOME NEWS.

THEY REALLY MUST BE JOKING!

THE TOP BRASS WEREN'T. RALPH HAD NEEDLED SOMEBODY WITH HIS MANY REQUESTS FOR A TRANSFER AND HAD BEEN POSTED SIMPLY TO GET HIM OUT OF THE WAY.

I'M NOT HAVING IT! I'M GOING AS HIGH AS NEED BE TO HAVE THIS CANCELLED!

THAT DIDN'T HELP. TWO DAYS LATER, RALPH GRUMPILY REPORTED TO AN INTELLIGENCE CORPS BASE IN A GERMAN TOWN, MANNED BY COLIN AND MIKE, THOSE EXPERTS AT SWANNING ABOUT BEHIND ENEMY LINES.

THIS CAN'T BE WHERE I FIND LIEUTENANT TAIT, CAN IT?

THAT INFO MIGHT BE RESTRICTED, SIR, DEPENDING ON WHO WANTS TO KNOW.

THE REPLY RAISED RALPH'S BLOOD PRESSURE A FEW NOTCHES, BUT HE DULY PRESENTED HIS DOCUMENTS AND COLIN CLEARED A CHAIR FOR HIM.

TAKE A PEW, SIR. THE LIEUTENANT WILL BE BACK SOON. STILL CAN'T TAKE SECURITY FOR GRANTED. THE NAZIS ARE A CUNNING BUNCH.

IS HE REALLY SERIOUS OR HAVING ME ON?

NOT IMPRESSED BY WHO HE JUDGED AS DESK-BOUND DODGERS AND TOTALLY UNAWARE OF THEIR FORAYS INTO GERMAN TERRITORY, RALPH WAITED IMPATIENTLY UNTIL ALFRED RETURNED.

AH, YOU'LL BE LIEUTENANT LOACH. WELCOME TO MY LITTLE OUTFIT.

YOU MEAN THERE ARE JUST THE THREE OF YOU?

THE INTELLIGENCE OFFICER NODDED.

SUITS US BETTER THAT WAY. A TIGHT TEAM. I REPORT TO H.Q., OF COURSE, BUT THEY LEAVE US TO CARRY OUT WHAT ORDERS WE HAVE.

WELL, I DON'T INTEND TO BE AROUND HERE FOR LONG. I'M WAITING FOR A POSTING TO THE FRONT LINE.

THE CHAMPAGNE WAS SOON FOUND. THE FOUR RAISED THEIR TIN MUGS IN A TOAST, ALTHOUGH RALPH'S DISAPPOINTMENT BLUNTED ANY JUBILATION HE MIGHT HAVE FELT.

HERE'S TO GETTING THIS FAR IN ONE PIECE.

I'LL DRINK TO THAT, SIR.

SO IT'S ALL OVER THEN? BUT WHO'S GOING TO BRING THOSE NAZI THUGS WE KEEP HEARING ABOUT TO JUSTICE?

ALFRED ANSWERED CALMLY.

OH THAT'LL BECOME A PRIORITY NOW. VERY FEW WILL ESCAPE THE NET IF WE CAN HELP IT.

AFTER A WHILE RALPH LEFT THE H.Q. FOR HIS NEW BILLET. THOUGH HE HAD SAID NOTHING ABOUT THE INCIDENT, HE WAS THINKING OF THE DEVIL WHO HAD SLAIN HIS MEN AND WOUNDED HIM. HE HAD NO FAITH IN MEN LIKE HIS NEW COMRADES TO BRING HIM TO JUSTICE.

PORING OVER MAPS AND PUSHING PAPERS ABOUT... WHAT GOOD IS THAT GOING TO DO ANYBODY? HOW'S THAT GOING TO CATCH ANY NAZI WAR CRIMINALS?

BY NOW, THERE WAS MUCH TALK THAT THE STRENGTH OF THE GERMAN FORCES IN AND AROUND ARNHEM HAD BEEN BADLY UNDERESTIMATED.

STILL STINGING FROM THE PAINS OF HIS OWN INVOLVEMENT, HE WAS READY TO PIN THE BLAME, UNJUSTLY IN MANY WAYS, ON INTELLIGENCE-GATHERING FALLING SHORT.

RALPH FELT BITTER THAT THERE HAD BEEN NO MENTION OF TREES POSING A PROBLEM IN HIS BRIEFINGS. HE SEEMED TO OVERLOOK THE FACT THAT HE AND HIS MEN HAD LANDED WELL AWAY FROM THEIR ALLOTTED DROPPING ZONE.

ALL THESE FACTORS COMBINED TO MAKE HIM WANT TO HAVE AS LITTLE TO DO WITH HIS NEW UNIT AS POSSIBLE.

WITHIN THE WEEK HE HAD ANOTHER REMINDER OF ARNHEM — HE HAD TO ENDURE ANOTHER FLIGHT IN A DOUGLAS DAKOTA. ALFRED'S TEAM HAD BEEN ORDERED TO BATTERED BERLIN, NOW CARVED UP INTO FOUR SECTORS — BRITISH, FRENCH, AMERICAN AND RUSSIAN.

OUR JOB IS TO KEEP TABS ON ANY SUSPECT GERMANS AND ALSO VET THE RUSSIANS. THEY MIGHT NOT BE QUITE SO FRIENDLY NOW, LIEUTENANT.

BUT SURELY THE SOVIETS ARE STILL OUR ALLIES?

TALKING ABOUT ANYTHING WAS BETTER FOR RALPH THAN
THINKING ABOUT HIS PREVIOUS FRIGHTENING FLIGHT IN A DAK.

ON PAPER MAYBE, BUT I THINK THEIR AGENDA MIGHT BE TO ROUND UP AS MANY TOP NAZI SCIENTISTS AS THEY CAN TO WORK FOR THEM, BEATING US AND THE YANKS TO IT.

ALLIES TURNING INTO ENEMIES...

NOT SO MUCH ENEMIES AS RIVALS. AT LEAST SO FAR.

SO MUCH FOR ALL THAT EFFORT TO WIN THE WAR.

WELL, THAT WAS WORTH IT, BUT GATHERING INTELLIGENCE DOESN'T HALT JUST BECAUSE THE BULLETS STOP FLYING. GOT TO STAY AHEAD OF THE GAME.

RALPH THOUGHT THOSE WORDS OVER AND THEY SEEMED
TO CONFIRM WHAT HE HAD BEEN THINKING ALL ALONG.

IT'S LIKE SOME GREAT GAME
TO THESE INTELLIGENCE
BLOKES. THEORIES GALORE
BUT IT'S STILL THE POOR
FOOT SOLDIER WHO LIVES OR
DIES BY THEIR GEN. JUST LIKE
AT ARNHEM.

RALPH KNEW LITTLE OR NOTHING ABOUT
WHAT THE INTELLIGENCE CORPS HAD DONE
OVER THE YEARS IN THEIR ATTEMPT TO REDUCE
CASUALTIES. BACK IN THE NAPOLEONIC WAR...

...WHEN THEY WERE KNOWN AS "EXPLORING OFFICERS",
THEY HAD RISKED ALL TO ALERT HIGH COMMAND TO
FRENCH TROOP MOVEMENTS AND STRENGTHS.

LATER IN THAT SAME CENTURY, DURING
THE BOER WARS IN SOUTH AFRICA, THEY
HAD COME FROM THE SHADOWS AS
RIMINGTON'S GUIDES, THE CORPS OF GUIDES,
DAMANT'S HORSE, THE CORPS OF SCOUTS...

...A CONFUSING LIST OF NAMES BUT
ALL HAD ONE GOAL...TO COLLECT AND
ANALYSE VITAL MILITARY INTELLIGENCE.

THE FIRST WORLD WAR SAW THE CORPS ROOTING OUT ENEMY AGENTS
BEHIND BRITISH LINES WHILE THEMSELVES SLIPPING INTO HOSTILE
TERRITORY TO COLLECT GEN ON TROOP MOVEMENTS AND THE LIKE...

...AND WHEN THEY WEREN'T EXAMINING VITAL
AERIAL VIEWS OF THE BATTLEFIELDS TAKEN BY THE
NEW RECONNAISSANCE AIRCRAFT, THEY WERE ALSO
DRAWING INTELLIGENCE FROM MONITORING GERMAN
RADIO COMMUNICATIONS ON THE GROUND.

NOW ALFRED'S UNIT WAS TO PLY A SIMILAR TRADE IN THEIR NEW BERLIN BASE — A CELLAR WHICH HAD BEEN THE OFFICE OF SOME NAZI ORGANISATION. THE SHELLING AND BOMBING OF THE CITY HAD LEFT THE PLACE LADEN WITH DUST.

COULDN'T WE HAVE GOT A BETTER PLACE THAN THIS?

NO, NOT MANY DIGS LEFT WITH ROOFS ON THEM AND WE'VE A GOOD SOLID ONE HERE.

RALPH, HIS SPIRITS LOW, HAD AGAIN BEGUN TO CAST HIS MIND BACK AND WONDER HOW HE MIGHT HAVE FARED HAD HE BEEN GIVEN THE CHANCE TO FIGHT.

I'LL NEVER KNOW NOW, I BET, AND THESE PAPER-PUSHING PUPPETS I'M LANDED WITH WILL BE LUCKY TO NET ONE WANTED NAZI.

HE WAS ABOUT TO MOVE ON WHEN HE SAW ALFRED SURFACE JUST AS A BURLY COMMANDO MAJOR PASSED.

LIEUTENANT TAIT! GOOD TO SEE YOU. AFTER THE SCRAPES WE WERE IN TOGETHER I'M A BIT SURPRISED YOU SURVIVED THE WAR. PLEASED, THOUGH!

YES, WE DID PUSH OUR LUCK A LITTLE, MAJOR. CARE TO GO FIND A BEER?

THE EXCHANGE PUZZLED RALPH UNTIL HE REMEMBERED THE INTELLIGENCE OFFICERS WHO HAD OFTEN OVERSEEN HIS PARA TRAINING.

LIEUTENANT TAIT MUST'VE BEEN WORKING WITH THE COMMANDOS BEFORE THEY WENT ON OPS. HE WOULDN'T BE UP TO MUCH ELSE, I SUSPECT.

RALPH COULDN'T HAVE BEEN MORE WRONG. ALBERT HAD BEEN ON MORE THAN ONE COMMANDO RAID PRIOR TO D-DAY, COLLECTING INFORMATION FROM LOCALS ABOUT TIDES AND DETERMINING WHAT WEIGHT OF FIGHTING VEHICLES CERTAIN BEACHES COULD TAKE.

WE'VE HAD A LUCKY RUN SO FAR, SO FINGERS CROSSED.

ALBERT'S THOUGHT WAS SCARCELY A SECOND OLD WHEN A BLINDING LIGHT CAUGHT THEM COLD. THE CREW OF AN ENEMY HALF-TRACK PARKED BY THE NO-GO ZONE CLOSE TO THE WATERLINE HAD HEARD THE SLIGHTEST OF NOISE FROM THE RAIDERS.

WE KNOW SOMEBODY IS OUT THERE! SHOW YOURSELVES OR WE OPEN FIRE! VITE!

34

SUSPECTING SOME LOCAL FISHERMEN IGNORING THE CURFEW TO CATCH A BUMPER CROP, THE ENEMY N.C.O. HAD CALLED OUT IN FRENCH. ALFRED, DITCHING HIS CAP, ROSE TO REPLY IN THE SAME LANGUAGE, ONLY HIS HEAD SHOWING.

PARDON, MONSIEUR, BUT WE NEED TO FEED OUR FAMILIES...

DUMMKOPF, YOU HAVE BEEN WARNED OFTEN ENOUGH!

THE GERMANS RELAXED BUT THE LIEUTENANT'S PLAY-ACTING HAD ANOTHER PURPOSE. IT ALLOWED THE COMMANDOS TO AVOID A FIRE-FIGHT AND OUTFLANK THE ENEMY INSTEAD...

...TO STRIKE — SILENT AND DEADLY.

GOOD INTELLIGENCE WORK DEMANDS THAT YOU NEED TO KNOW ALL THE FACTS AND NOT JUMP TO CONCLUSIONS.

RALPH HAD FAILED ON BOTH COUNTS, COMING UP WITH THE ANSWER WHICH SUITED HIS ASSUMPTIONS BUT WAS FAR FROM THE TRUTH.

THE NEXT FEW WEEKS PASSED SLOWLY FOR RALPH. THEY WERE SPENT WATCHING "PERSONS OF INTEREST"...

...OR LISTENING IN FOR SUSPICIOUS RADIO SIGNALS PICKED UP ON CERTAIN FREQUENCIES.

I'M GOING SLOWLY MAD DOING THIS. THERE'S NO CHANCE NOW OF AVENGING ANY OF MY LADS.

THAT THE SITUATION IRKED HIM SHOWED IN HIS ATTITUDE. HE WAS SURLY AND UNCOMMUNICATIVE WITH THE OTHERS. FINALLY, WHILE CHANGING SHIFTS ON A SURVEILLANCE DETAIL, ARTHUR TOOK THE BULL BY THE HORNS.

LOOK, YOU'RE STUCK WITH US FOR THE TIME BEING, SO YOU'D BEST MAKE THE MOST OF IT. WE ALL KNOW YOU WANT A TRANSFER BUT YOU'LL NEVER GET ONE IF YOU KEEP THIS UP.

I DIDN'T THINK ANY OF THEM WERE PAYING ME THE SLIGHTEST NOTICE!

MY TEAM DESERVES SOME RESPECT, YOU KNOW. IT WAS A VERY HAIRY WAR FOR EVERY ONE OF US, NOT JUST BLOKES LIKE YOU. ALL OF US — AND I MEAN ALL — WERE IN SOME VERY TIGHT SPOTS.

HE'S GIVING IT BOTH BARRELS NOW...AND HE'S NOT JOKING. MAYBE THEY WERE AT THE SHARP END AFTER ALL. IT'S PROBABLY BEST NOT TO SAY ANYTHING RIGHT NOW.

THE CHASTENED PARA NODDED AND SLIPPED AWAY WITH A TANGLE OF FRESH THOUGHTS TUMBLING INTO HIS MIND.

BY NEXT MORNING, RALPH HAD REALISED THAT HIS ONLY CHANCE OF GETTING BACK TO HIS OLD UNIT WAS BY PLAYING THE GAME AND SHOWING THE OTHERS HE WAS SERIOUS. THE CHANCE SOON CAME WHEN ALFRED IDENTIFIED A GERMAN OF INTEREST.

MAX MULLER ...GOES BY THE NAME WEBER NOW. A CIVIL SERVANT BY HIS PAPERS BUT THEY'RE FALSE. HE WAS A RUTHLESS SENIOR GESTAPO OFFICER.

NOW ORGANISING SAFE ROUTES OUT OF GERMANY TO SOUTH AMERICA FOR WANTED NAZI TOERAGS. WE WANT TO SPEAK TO HIM.

THE SUSPECT WAS TAILED A FEW NIGHTS LATER AND LED THE SHADOWING TEAM FOR SOME MILES BEFORE ENTERING BERLIN'S SOVIET-CONTROLLED SECTOR.

IS IT WISE TO GO IN THERE AFTER HIM?

PROBABLY NOT, RALPH, BUT LET'S JUST MOVE IN A LITTLE...

...IF THE RUSSKIES SPOT US, WE CAN ALWAYS SAY WE GOT LOST. THAT'S PROVIDED THEY DON'T OPEN FIRE FIRST, OF COURSE. VERY TOUCHY THESE DAYS, I'VE HEARD.

WHAT THE HECK, LET'S DO IT.

THEIR PREY HAD BARELY COVERED A FEW MORE PACES BEFORE HE SCURRIED TO COVER. SOVIET SECURITY FORCE SOLDIERS OF THE N.K.V.D. HAD APPEARED, PPSH 41 SUB-MACHINE GUNS BLAZING AS THEY TARGETED A BUILDING.

THE IVANS MUST HAVE FOUND OUT ABOUT THE SAFE HOUSE!

SOME OF THOSE INSIDE, ALL FORMERLY HIGH-RANKING NAZI OFFICERS, TRIED TO GET AWAY, BUT THE RUSSIANS — AND THEIR BULLETS — WERE READY FOR THEM.

AAGH!

NO ESCAPE THIS WAY, NAZIS!

SCARED, MULLER RAN BACK THE WAY HE HAD COME, OUT OF THE SOVIET ZONE.

THIS IS NO PLACE TO HANG ABOUT TONIGHT.

MORE HASTE, LESS SPEED, THEY SAY. WITH MIKE WAITING BY MULLER'S ESCAPE ROUTE, THE FUGITIVE WAS SOON MAKING NO SPEED.

OUT COLD WITHOUT A SOUND. PERFECT.

RALPH WAS VERY IMPRESSED WITH — AND A LITTLE SURPRISED AT — THE CORPORAL'S HANDIWORK. ALFRED WAS STILL KEEPING AN EYE ON THE SOVIETS.

LOOKS LIKE OUR RUSSIAN ALLIES HAD SOME HELP FROM AN INFORMER.

ANYONE WE MIGHT RECOGNISE? LET ME SEE...

THE RUSSIAN SNATCH SQUAD HAD OBVIOUSLY NO WISH TO TAKE ANY PRISONERS. THE CIVILIAN CO-OPERATING WITH THEM WAS APPARENTLY ON VERY GOOD TERMS WITH THE RUSSIANS.

I SEE WHAT YOU MEAN. THEY'RE WORKING HAND IN GLOVE WITH THAT BLOKE. HE LOOKS VERY CONFIDENT ABOUT IT TOO.

AS HE SPOKE, THE TONE OF RALPH'S VOICE CHANGED FROM CALM TO SHOCKED.

I KNOW HIM ...HE'S THE ONE WHO EXECUTED MY MEN AND SHOT ME!

QUIET, KEEP IT DOWN...

RALPH HAD SPOKEN MORE LOUDLY THAN WAS WISE. THE N.K.V.D. LIEUTENANT AND HIS INFORMER HAD TURNED TO LOOK TOWARDS THE HIDDEN BRITISH AS THOUGH ALERTED BY A NOISE.

I CAN'T SEE ANYTHING. POSSIBLY A SCAVENGING RAT.

AND NOT THE TWO-LEGGED VARIETY. WE'VE DEALT WITH THEM ALREADY TONIGHT. NO SMALL THANKS TO YOU, SHADOW MAN.

42

THE CALLOUS TURNCOAT TOOK ONE LAST LOOK AT HIS FALLEN FORMER COMRADES. THERE WAS NO PITY IN HIS FACE.

FOR NOW I LIVE IN THE SHADOWS, BUT NOT FOR MUCH LONGER. NEIN, NOT FOR MUCH LONGER.

SOON AFTER THE SOVIETS HAD GONE, THE BRITISH AND THEIR PRISONER SLIPPED AWAY. RALPH'S MIND WAS IN TURMOIL.

I'M SURE IT WAS THAT MURDERING THUG! I'D BET ON IT!

ALL RIGHT, BUT GO EASY UNTIL WE'RE BACK AT BASE. WE CAN TALK IT THROUGH THEN.

43

THEIR PRISONER WAS LOCKED AWAY, STILL OUT COLD, BEFORE THE OTHERS GATHERED TO HEAR WHAT THE PARA OFFICER HAD TO SAY.

THAT'S ONE FACE I WILL NEVER FORGET. WHEN WE LANDED BACK IN 'FORTY-FOUR NEAR ARNHEM...

LOOK, DON'T DWELL ON THAT. WE'RE AWARE OF THE EXECUTIONS YOU WERE IN THE MIDDLE OF AND SO ON.

RALPH WAS STUNNED TO A SILENCE FOR A MOMENT.

YOU KNOW ALL ABOUT THAT?

WOULDN'T BE MUCH OF AN INTELLIGENCE UNIT IF WE DIDN'T RUN A BACKGROUND CHECK ON YOU AS A MATTER OF COURSE. WE JUST WONDERED HOW LONG YOU WOULD KEEP IT TO YOURSELF.

THAT INFORMATION TOOK RALPH'S BREATH AWAY ONCE MORE, BUT ALFRED PLOUGHED ON, STICKING TO THE PRESENT, NOT THE PAST.

THE POINT IS, WE'VE IDENTIFIED A POSSIBLE WAR CRIMINAL, AND NOW WE NEED TO DIG OUT HIS NAME, RANK AND NUMBER.

HOW COME HE'S WORKING WITH THE SOVIETS? THEY SURELY DON'T TAKE KINDLY TO HIS KIND.

AH, BUT HE MAY BE USING A FALSE IDENTITY TO FOOL THEM. OUR PRISONER MIGHT BE ABLE TO HELP.

AH, YES, BUT WILL HE EVER COME TO?

MIKE WAS ALREADY ORGANISING AN EARLY MORNING WAKE-UP CALL.

RISE AND SHINE, JERRY!

AARGH ...SCHWEIN!

THEIR CATCH, NOW TRYING TO MAKE ANY LIVING HE COULD IN HIS DEVASTATED HOME TOWN, OWNED UP ABOUT HIS PAST WHEN PRESENTED WITH THE FACTS BY THE BRITISH.

I HAD GONE TO GUIDE THE MEN IN THAT HOUSE INTO THE BRITISH SECTOR, BUT THE IVANS SHOWED UP FIRST.

SO YOU WERE LEADING THEM ON THEIR FIRST STEP ON THE ESCAPE LINE TO ITALY THEN? WHAT ABOUT YOUR KAMERAD WHO'S SO COSY WITH THE N.K.V.D.?

I HAVE NEVER SEEN THAT MAN BEFORE — EITHER DURING THE WAR OR AFTERWARDS. HE IS A STRANGER TO ME.

WELL, YOU'RE NO LONGER ANY USE TO US THEN. WE'LL PASS YOU ON...TO THE RUSSKIES.

THEY MAY NOT LOOK AFTER YOU QUITE AS WELL AS US, BUT YOU PROBABLY KNOW THAT ALREADY.

HE WENT OFF ON LEAVE TO BREMEN MORE SATISFIED THAN HE HAD FELT FOR A WHILE. UNKNOWN TO HIM, HIS INTELLIGENCE OPPOS WERE NOT LETTING LANDT'S TRAIL GO COLD. NOR WERE THEY STICKING TO COMBING THROUGH DOCUMENTS.

HE SEEMS QUITE AT HOME IN THE U.S SECTOR AS WELL AS THE RUSSIAN ONE.

I SUSPECT HE'S PLAYING ONE SIDE AGAINST THE OTHER. MAYBE HE'S ON OUR BOOKS TOO.

A PASSING AMERICAN OFFICER CLEARLY KNEW LANDT AND PAUSED TO CHAT AMIABLY. MIKE AND COLIN TOOK IT ALL IN.

THAT'S MAJOR BARTLETT. HE'S IN THE SAME LINE AS US. LOOKS LIKE OUR NAZI SHAPE-SHIFTER IS CHUMMING IN WITH ALL AND SUNDRY.

THE CRAFTY SCHEMER CERTAINLY WAS WORKING WITH BOTH SIDES, THOUGH NEITHER THE AMERICANS NOR THE RUSSIANS HAD ANY INKLING OF THIS. HIS MAIN GOAL, AS EVER, WAS SELF-PRESERVATION.

THE SCHWEIN PAY WELL. SOON I WILL HAVE ENOUGH MONEY TO SLIP THROUGH ITALY AND TAKE A BOAT TO ARGENTINA FOR A QUIETER LIFE WITH MY KAMERADEN ALREADY THERE.

A PASSAGE UNDER THE RUBBLE LED INTO THE SKELETON OF A FACTORY WHERE THE SQUAD OF LANDT'S FORMER UNIT — WHO ACTED AS HIS BODYGUARD — HID OUT.

WELCOME BACK, HERR STURM...

MENTION NO RANKS, DUMMKOPF! IF ANYBODY ELSE HEARD, A SLIP LIKE THAT COULD GIVE US AWAY!

EVERY ONE OF THIS SMALL BAND OF EXTREMISTS WOULD RECEIVE LITTLE MERCY IF THE ALLIES NETTED THEM...

...BUT NONE OF THEM REALISED THEIR LEADER INTENDED TO ABSCOND, LEAVING THEM HIGH AND DRY.

TWO MORE GOOD PAYDAYS AND I'LL BE MOVING OUT. I'VE HAD ENOUGH OF THIS SQUALOR.

RALPH WAS SOON BACK FROM LEAVE, SUSPECTING THAT NOTHING MUCH WOULD HAVE BEEN DONE ABOUT LANDT. ALFRED'S CHEERFUL LOOK ALERTED HIM THAT THINGS MIGHT NOT BE AS HE EXPECTED.

AH, GOOD TO SEE YOU AGAIN. WE'VE BEEN RATHER BUSY ON YOUR BEHALF.

WHY DOES THAT MAKE ME NERVOUS?

THEY SET OFF IN THE UNIT'S JEEP, ALFRED'S ERRATIC DRIVING DOING LITTLE TO CALM RALPH'S NERVES. THE PARA OFFICER SOON BEGAN TO FORGET THE CRUNCHING GEAR CHANGES AS HE LISTENED TO WHAT THE INTELLIGENCE OFFICER HAD TO SAY.

...TO RECAP, OUR TARGET IS A THOROUGHLY NASTY PIECE OF WORK WHO IS PLAYING EVERY FACTION HE CAN AGAINST THE OTHERS. AND, WE SUSPECT, HE'S PREPARING TO BOLT.

IF HE'S HOLED UP IN THE YANK SECTOR, WHY NOT TELL THEM AND THEY'LL NAB HIM?

THE WEARY TONE OF ALFRED'S VOICE MADE IT CLEAR THAT HE WAS NOT TOO HAPPY ABOUT SUCH A MOVE.

OH, I'M SURE THEY WOULD, AND THEN LET HIM SLIP AWAY UNHARMED TO CARRY ON HIS MURKY WORK FOR THEM.

SO WHY NOT KIDNAP HIM AND HAUL HIM BACK INTO THE BRITISH SECTOR?

THAT COULD LEAD TO WHAT'S TERMED AS A DIPLOMATIC INCIDENT. NOT A GOOD IDEA.

SO HE'S UNTOUCHABLE?

HE MIGHT THINK HE IS, BUT PRIDE OFTEN DOES COME BEFORE A FALL.

A FEW NIGHTS LATER, THE BRITISH TEAM MET SOME OF THEIR RUSSIAN COUNTERPARTS ON THE FRINGES OF THE SOVIET AND BRITISH SECTORS. ALFRED HAD BROUGHT A SHEAF OF DOCUMENTS WHICH HE HANDED OVER TO AN N.K.V.D. CAPTAIN.

DOES LIEUTENANT TAIT SPEAK RUSSIAN AS WELL AS GERMAN THEN?

YES. PLUS FRENCH...ITALIAN TOO AT A PUSH.

RALPH WAS ALL EAGER TO ASK QUESTIONS WHEN THE MEETING BROKE UP, BUT ALFRED WAS NOT READY TO SPEAK FREELY JUST YET.

AREN'T YOU GOING TO TELL ME WHAT THAT WAS ALL ABOUT?

HAVE PATIENCE, OLD SPORT. CARELESS TALK COSTS LIVES AND ALL THAT...JUST JOKING. YOU'LL SOON SEE FOR YOURSELF ANYWAY. MAYBE YOU'LL EVEN WORK IT OUT BEFORE THAT.

WORK IT OUT? FAT CHANCE OF THAT WITH THE TORTUROUS WAY THIS LOT'S MINDS WORK.

RALPH, HOPING IT WOULD BE WORTHWHILE, SETTLED FOR WAIT AND SEE.

BEFORE THE END OF THE WEEK, TWO AMERICAN M.P.s — DUBBED SNOWDROPS BECAUSE OF THE WHITE COVERS ON THEIR HELMETS — WERE ENDING A ROUTINE PATROL WHEN THEY CAME UNDER FIRE.

SOME KRAUTS DON'T KNOW IT'S ALL OVER!

MILITARY POLICE

WELL, IT SOON WILL BE IF WE SPOT THE SON OF A GUN!

THE YANKS RATTLED OFF A FEW SHOTS AT WHERE THEY THOUGHT THE FIRE HAD COME FROM.

I BET THEY'RE IN THAT BUSTED FACTORY.

TOO SOON TO TELL YET...

NOT REALISING THAT THE M.P.s HAD NO IDEA WHERE THE SINGLE SHOT HAD COME FROM, ONE OF THE RENEGADES HOLED UP IN THE BUILDING FROM WHICH LANDT RAN HIS OPERATIONS REPLIED IN KIND.

THE SCHWEIN ARE ON TO US! BACK ME UP!

THE SHOOTING ATTRACTED THE ATTENTION OF THE CREW OF AN AMERICAN M24 CHAFFEE TANK.

WANT ANY HELP HERE, FELLAS?

IS GERONIMO AN APACHE?

THE FIRST U.S. ARMOURED VEHICLE TO ROLL ON TO GERMAN SOIL ON THE EASTERN BANK OF THE RHINE, THE CHAFFEE PACKED A 75MM MAIN GUN. ITS GUNNER WAS HAPPY TO ASSIST, EVEN IF IT WAS FOR M.P.s.

PUNCH MORE HOLES IN THOSE WALLS!

THE LIGHTER GUNFIRE HAD ALREADY ROUSED LANDT, BUT AN AMERICAN SHELL AIRING HIS BEDROOM WAS STILL UNEXPECTED.

HIMMEL, WHAT IS GOING ON?

A SHOT WAS FIRED, AND THEN THE AMERIKANERS CAME AT US OUT OF NOWHERE!

THE STURMBANNFUHRER'S ANGER WAS NOT ONLY RESERVED FOR THE ENEMIES OF THE REICH.

JA, BUT WHICH OF YOU SCHWEIN WAS STUPID ENOUGH TO LOOSE OFF THAT FIRST BULLET?

IT WAS NOT ME, HERR...

THE S.S. MAN'S LAST WORDS DIED IN HIS THROAT WHEN ANOTHER 75MM SHELL SLAMMED INTO THE BUILDING AND AN AVALANCHE OF MASONRY CRASHED INTO THE ROOM.

MEIN GOTT ...I MUST GET OUT OF HERE...

LEAVING THE OTHERS TO THEIR DOOM WITHOUT A SECOND THOUGHT, THE NAZI BRUTE CLUTCHED HIS BRIEFCASE AND HIS LUGER. AS THE AMERICAN ASSAULT CONTINUED, HE CLATTERED DOWN TOWARDS THE BASEMENT.

IT'S TIME TO HEAD FOR ITALY NOW. I PROBABLY HAVE ENOUGH CASH WITHOUT ANOTHER PAYDAY, ANYWAY.

HE LEFT USING THE SAME SECRET WAY HE HAD ENTERED BY, PAUSING CAUTIOUSLY TO ENSURE THAT HE HAD NOT BEEN SPOTTED.

AS LONG AS THEY CARRY ON FIGHTING BEHIND ME NO-ONE WILL HAVE EYES OUT FOR ME.

BUT WATCHFUL EYES WERE ON HIM IN FACT, CHARTING HIS EVERY CHANGE OF DIRECTION.

SHOULDN'T WE TRY TO TAKE HIM DOWN?

NO, THAT'S NOT THE PLAN.

WATCHING ALL OF THIS WERE ALFRED AND HIS SQUAD. LOOKING AT HIS FELLOW LIEUTENANT'S SMILE, RALPH REALISED THAT THEY HAD NOT COME UPON THIS SKIRMISH BY CHANCE.

I'D GIVE ANYTHING TO WRING THAT RAT'S NECK!

TOTALLY JUSTIFIED BUT TOO EXTREME. TOO MANY QUESTIONS WOULD BE ASKED AND, SINCE LANDT DOES SEEM TO BE AN ASSET TO THE YANKS, YOU'D BE IN VERY HOT WATER.

YES, BUT HE'S HEADING INTO THE SOVIET SECTOR. WE CAN'T GO AFTER HIM THERE AND HE'LL BE FREE TO CARRY ON WORKING FOR THEM. MAYBE EVEN GET OUT OF GERMANY.

WHICH WAS EXACTLY WHAT THE NAZI WAS THINKING TOO.

I MIGHT DO ONE MORE JOB FOR THE BOLSHEVIKS AFTER ALL AND THEN HEAD SOUTH TO SAFETY.

FROM NOWHERE THE WOODEN STOCK OF A RUSSIAN PPSH 41 SUB-MACHINE GUN HELD BY AN N.K.V.D. SOLDIER SLAMMED INTO LANDT'S SHOULDER.

AAGH!

BE STILL, GERMANSKI!

THE EYES OF THE SOVIET SECURITY OFFICER WERE AS COLD AS THE WATERS OF THE SIBERIAN RIVER HE HAD GROWN UP BESIDE.

YOU HAVE BEEN USEFUL BUT WE DO HAVE LIMITS ON WHO WE WORK WITH. I HAVE BEEN GIVEN INFORMATION REVEALING THAT YOU AND YOUR SQUAD EXECUTED MANY OF OUR SENIOR OFFICERS CAPTURED WHEN OUR MOTHERLAND WAS INVADED.

NEIN, THAT IS NOT THE CASE...

THE NAZI'S CAPTORS WERE NOT LISTENING TO HIS PLEADING. A GRIM INTERROGATION AWAITED HIM, A SINGLE BULLET TO THE BACK OF THE NECK AND AN UNMARKED GRAVE THE INEVITABLE OUTCOME. RALPH, HOWEVER, WAS TAKEN ABACK.

ISN'T THAT THE SAME N.K.V.D. OFFICER YOU MET WITH SOME DAYS BACK, ALFRED?

IF YOU SAY SO, OLD CHUM. THESE RUSSKIS ALL LOOK ALIKE TO ME.

THE PARA LIEUTENANT BEGAN TO GRASP THAT ALFRED HAD SHOPPED LANDT TO THE N.K.V.D.

YOU KNEW THE YANKS WOULD GO EASY ON THAT THUG, MAYBE WAIT UNTIL THE FUSS HAD DIED DOWN AND LET HIM OUT AGAIN.

ARE YOU SUGGESTING THAT OUR SOVIET ALLIES WILL BE LESS FORGIVING? THAT'S A BIT NAUGHTY.

ALFRED'S HABIT OF ANSWERING A QUESTION WITH ANOTHER QUESTION NO LONGER CONFUSED RALPH. HE CARRIED ON.

YOU SET THIS WHOLE THING UP TO GET LANDT INTO THE HANDS YOU KNEW WOULD BE MOST UNFORGIVING. YOU PULLED THE STRINGS AND CONFUSED THE LOT OF THEM, ME INCLUDED!

A CRAFTY ITALIAN ONCE SAID THAT THE END JUSTIFIES THE MEANS. I THINK IT DOES IN THIS CASE...AND THERE MIGHT JUST BE THE MAKING OF AN INTELLIGENCE OFFICER IN YOU YET.

RALPH WASN'T SURE IF THAT WAS GENUINE PRAISE OR SIMPLY FLATTERY TO APPEASE HIM, BUT WHEN THEY SAW THE SURRENDER OF THE LAST OF THE S.S., HE CHEERFULLY POINTED OUT THAT ALFRED'S SCHEME MIGHT NOT HAVE WORKED BUT FOR CHANCE.

YOU WERE LUCKY THAT ONE OF THE NAZIS LOOSED OFF A NERVOUS SHOT AND MADE LANDT BREAK COVER AND RUN.

YES, IT WOULD SEEM THAT GOOD FORTUNE SMILED ON US. BETTER HEAD BACK TO BASE NOW.

ALBERT LED THE WAY BACK TO THE JEEP, COLIN AND MIKE FOLLOWING WITH RALPH.

WE KNEW WE COULD HELP YOU SETTLE THINGS IN THE END, SIR.

IT JUST TOOK SOME SETTING UP.

AND A STROKE OF LUCK WITH A TRIGGER-HAPPY JERRY OPENING FIRE, BUT I'LL NOT GRUDGE YOU ON THAT SCORE.

THE SERGEANT AND CORPORAL GAVE NOTHING AWAY, AND RALPH DID NOT SPOT THE TARPAULIN-WRAPPED WEHRMACHT MAUSER 98k RIFLE SECURED AT THE REAR OF THE JEEP...

...WHICH HAD BEEN FIRED BY COLIN TO SPARK OFF THE GUNFIGHT WHICH HAD RESULTED IN LANDT BEING FLUSHED FROM COVER. THE M24 TURNING UP HAD BEEN AN UNEXPECTED AND WELCOME BONUS — NOTHING ELSE HAD BEEN LEFT TO CHANCE.

MAYBE ONE DAY RALPH WOULD LEARN THE TRUTH. IN THE MEANTIME HE WOULD TURN DOWN THE OFFER OF A RETURN TO HIS REGIMENT UNTIL HE HAD BETTER MASTERED THE TWISTS AND TURNS OF THE WORK DONE BY THE MOSTLY UNSUNG HEROES OF THE INTELLIGENCE CORPS.

IT IS NO SURPRISE THAT THEIR LATIN MOTTO TRANSLATES AS "KNOWLEDGE GIVES STRENGTH TO THE ARM" ...WHICH MIGHT LEAD TO A GENTLE TAP OR, IN THE EXTREME, A HAMMER BLOW. YOU HAVE BEEN WARNED...

INTELLIGENCE CORPS

**Commando**
**THE END**

# AIM FOR ACTION!

## Commando

**You've read one – Don't miss the others:**

### KNOW YOUR ENEMY

### ONE FALSE MOVE...

### APPOINTMENT IN CAIRO

### OPERATION DOUBLE BLUFF

## www.commandocomics.com

**CONTACT DETAILS** By post: Commando, D.C. Thomson & Co., Ltd, 80 Kingsway East, Dundee DD4 8SL
● email: editor@commandomag.com ● phone: **01382 223131**

**PROMOTIONS** promotions@dcthomson.co.uk
**SUBSCRIPTIONS** shop@dcthomson.co.uk
**SYNDICATION** syndication@dcthomson.co.uk
**CIRCULATION** circulation@dcthomson.co.uk

♻ **recycle**
When you have finished with this magazine please recycle it.

**For advertising please contact:**
Bryn Piper 020 7400 1050 bpiper@dcthomson.co.uk
Amy-Louise Reeves 020 7400 1047 areeves@dcthomson.co.uk

**Licensing:**
start.licensing@btinternet.com

**COMPETITION RULES** Employees of D.C Thomson and their families are not eligible for prizes.
The Editor's decision is final and no correspondence will be entered into.

Distributed by Marketforce, Blue Fin Building,
110 Southwark Street, London, SE1 0SU.

Tel: +44 (0) 20 3148 3300
Fax: +44 (0) 203 148 8106
Website: www.marketforce.co.uk

DC Thomson Published in Great Britain by **D.C. Thomson & Co., Ltd.,**
80 Kingsway East, Dundee DD4 8SL. © D.C. Thomson & Co., Ltd., 2015